Cold Reading for Actors

Simple and Easy Building of Your Actor's Skill

By R.D. "Doc" Whitney

Acknowledgements

Much like medicine, acting is an art and actors, though they try, will never reach a pinnacle from which there is nothing left to learn. I would like to thank the many instructors, coaches, authors, students, and friends who have worked with me in my journey into the art of acting.

Also, a sincere thank you to my grammatical editor, Sara Sewell who has been able to do what I have consistently been unable to do: correct the english language.

A sincere thanks to my wife and children who have given me so many memories and experiences that I can use in my craft.

To my father Stanley and mother Elmay, thanks for helping me through those stormy formative years of adolescence.

TABLE OF CONTENTS

"The general who wins a battle makes many calculations in his temple before the battle is fought."

Sun Tzu

INTRODUCTION

COLD READ

Many people want to act in theater or film, and everyone has to start somewhere. There are many excellent classes, and I whole heartedly suggest that those who are serious about working professionally on stage, in the movies, or in front of the public take as many classes as possible.

For those just beginning in the profession, there are two major problems faced by most. First, quality classes are expensive and can wreck or totally destroy many budgets, and second, there is the element of time or, better put, not enough of it. Since most new actors work day jobs, many with families, it is not always convenient or possible to attend classes as often as needed.

This book is written to that end. Cold reading can be a new script just handed to you without prior knowledge or it can also mean that the actor is totally unprepared (reading cold) to deliver a believable audition or performance. This book is designed to provide you with a simple, easy method to practice your acting craft daily without the benefit of classes and/or an acting coach.

So, here we go:

Words are vocal sounds or visual graphics which convey meaning from one person to another. Used either alone or in phrases, conveyed meanings of words may transmit information that is either factual, fantasy or abstract.

Reading is the receiving, in words or visual graphics, the ideas and emotions of a person or persons. Simply stated, it is input.

Acting is conveying the meaning of those ideas and emotions transmitted by the first person (author) to the second person (actor) who then delivers those meanings (chosen by the actor or director) to a third person (audience).   This is output.

Most people prefer to read a book themselves rather than have someone flatly just recite the words from the page. While reading the book, the author's words are mixed with internal ideas, feelings and memories which bring the words to life.

In order for an actor to realistically convey the author or director's ideas, emotions, and feelings, an actor must first be aware of those emotions and feelings within himself. If you can't communicate to yourself the emotions which define the words you are reciting, how will you be able to communicate those feelings and emotions to someone else?

Cold reading is the exact same process except that it is usually on a moment's notice or with little time to rehearse that transmission.

PLUG-n-PLAY

The computer industry coined the term 'plug and play' for computer hardware or software that can be taken directly off the shelf, plugged into any computer with a compatible operating system and used immediately without extensive setup or programming. Within minutes you are playing the game.

Borrowing the term 'Plug-n-Play' from the computer industry, you are about to build your own plug and play cold reading system. With this system you plug pre-prepared emotions and feeling (software) that you have developed and you plug it into words and actions (hardware) that you or someone else has written or developed. Within minutes you are performing the scene.

Much like the tools a carpenter or mechanic carries in a tool box, your 'Plug-n-Play 'art set will be a group of tools (developed talents or skills) which you can use with almost no fore thought and can be substituted and used on any variety of situations and/or jobs (aka audition, cold reads, public speaking, business meetings, sales presentations, addressing juries, etc.)

Throughout human history, the great communicators are those individuals who can motivate and move the masses with their performances. Great generals motivate their troops to go into battle knowing quite well that they may die. Great jurist persuade juries of innocence or guilt, changing the lives of people forever. Great salesmen convince the public to give their hard earned money for products that will meet their needs and improve their lives. Great actors bring people to their feet with inspiring or poignant performances; performances that will educate, entertain, or stimulate new ideas and thoughts in those they are presented to.

Unlike a carpenter or mechanic's toolbox, which must be carried and stored until needed, your 'Plug-n-Play' art set will be built into your mind and soul making it always available to you 24/7 at will.

Acting is communication of emotions, thoughts and ideas. These are transmitted by your attitude, eyes, voice, face, body language, and movement. These are controlled by your brain. Your skill development of these talents will greatly enhance your cold reading abilities.

Every person is unique and each of us has unique talents. This booklet is not aimed at eliminating that uniqueness but building upon it. Depending on the situation and the needs of what you are trying to accomplish at the particular time you are trying to accomplish it will depend on which skills and techniques you will use.

KISS

Amateur or pro, you need to crawl before you can walk. You need to walk before you can run.

In an effort to K.I.S.S. (Keep It Simple Stupid) I've listed only a few common emotions, thoughts and ideas which you should know and be able to REPRODUCE from your own life on a moment's notice. Once you've developed your internal memories and feelings as they pertain to your own life, you will learn to switch the memories and feelings of your own life and hang them upon someone completely different (other actors.)

For example, let's say I hate my brother because he stole my girlfriend away from me back in high school. We're fine now but I still have that memory and have developed it and can feel all the pain and anger I had back then. Now I'm cast in a scene where my character hates my stage wife because she's cheating on me and my character feels as though she stole my love and honor and gave it away to someone else.

While delivering my lines from the script, I'll be thinking about and feeling how much I hate my brother. My brother, in my mind, is now the other actor I'm doing the scene with.

These are some skills (emotions) most any actor or communicator should have. These are not meant to be all inclusive and you can add to it as you grow in your competence or professional requirements.

Communicating (acting, sales, public presentation, etc.) is much like photography- the camera the photographer uses is not nearly as important as the photographer's talent. Many of the greatest photographs of the twentieth century were made using a simple box camera. Celebrated actor or beginner, you should strive to develop and be the best talent possible.

As a communicator, sharpen and hone each talent and emotion so that when you deliver your performance, regardless of where it is at or to whom it is delivered, it will bring life and meaning to your work.

This is not to say that you should deliver 'canned' performances. Certainly, if you have the availability and time to perfect a role, you should work and heighten your character nuances and actions. Always use all the tools available to you whether you have the time to rehearse and build them or not.

Cold reading skills are used so you can be ready and available to deliver any script anywhere, anytime, and successfully communicate the author or director's meaning. Anyone can just 'read' the words. Great talents 'deliver' them with all the heat and passion of real life.

As an added benefit, once you've developed your cold reading abilities, you can make different choices of which emotions and feelings you rehearse scripts with. Different choices may give you insight into your or your character's perspective.

START WITH BASICS

There are two activities necessary for you to build your 'Plug-n-Play' art set:

      1. PREPARATION

      2. PRACTICE

      The degree of your proficiency and the performance power and influence with which you will be able to create with your 'Plug-n-Play' art set will depend upon your time and effort committed to learning and practicing with your set.

      I suggest that you spend 15 to 30 minutes every day preparing and practicing your acting craft.

WARNING: Don't complicate your personal life by disclosing your most intimate secrets.

Hopefully, the memories, emotions and events you are going to remember and write out are really strong occurrences from your life, real feelings with blood and 'juice.' Because these are for YOU only, you should protect them from disclosure to anyone: yes, ANYONE!

I say this because your most vivid memories and thoughts can be painful, illegal, or downright embarrassing. Usually, the more painful, the more illegal, or the more embarrassing your thoughts and feelings, the easier it is for you, once you've learned to confine and use them, to communicate them to others hidden beneath the words of a script. Only you need to know what you are thinking about and what is really triggering the feelings the audience is seeing when any character you are portraying is performing.

FOR EXAMPLE:

Your high school sweetheart, someone that you absolutely love, suddenly, without any indication, breaks up with you and starts to go steady with your best friend. You feel the pain of loss, the anger of betrayal, the bitter sweetness of wanting revenge, the self pity and rationalizations you create for this happening to you.

There is a common thread of emotions and feelings that run through all of us humans regardless of national origin, language or nationality. It has been called by some authors the 'commonality of pain.' Your audience will inwardly identify with those feeling of loss and pain that you insert into your performance and that will attract their attention.

As my mother used to say, "A little rain falls into everyone's life." You want your audience to see and feel that 'rain' (or sunshine) in your character. They just won't know where or when it truly originated from.

There are two simple woodworking tools found in various forms worldwide: a hammer and a saw.

Just about anyone with at least one arm and hand can use any of these two tools. An unskilled beginner can use a hammer to drive nails and a saw to cut boards but the result will probably be less than perfect. On the other hand, a highly skilled carpenter can use these two simple tools to build fantastic projects.

While I would think there might be those who are born with the carpenter's gift of using these tools to perfection the first time they pick them up, it is more likely that there are a greater majority who will suck at first and only improve with practice.

Everyone, regardless of their station, can improve with practice and determination.

Hence, here is a mantra for those who, regardless of how high or how low they currently are, aspire to climb the success ladder to the pinnacle and build a powerful 'Plug-n-Play' communication skill set:

"If at first you don't succeed, keep sucking till you do."

B. J. Palmer

PREPARATION

Can you identify with or have experienced any of the listed below emotions in your own life?

Get into a darkened quiet place where you can let yourself float back to past memories from your life. Get comfortable. Close your eyes and breathe deeply.

For some this may not be easy but with patience and time most of us can identify events or moments that we felt some or all of these emotions.

Who was it?

What was it about?

Why did it happen?

Where was it at?

When was it?

Take your time with this exercise and fully investigate each emotion one at a time.

Most importantly, how did it make you feel?

For some, writing out notes about what memories you bring up from the mental depths can be helpful. Put words to those feelings. For now, just do short notes to help you remember the event. We'll go deeper and more into detail a little later.

CANNED DEFINITIONS

LOVE

Feel affection for, adore, worship, be in love with, be devoted to, care for, find irresistible, be keen on, be fond of

Opposite: hatred

EXAMPLE: When I walked into the room I saw her and couldn't take my eyes from her. It was like she was some ultra strong magnet and I was iron.

HATE

Abhorrence, detestation, hatred, odium, revulsion, disgust, extreme dislike

18

Opposite: love

EXAMPLE: The man had had 5 DUIs and he was drunk when he crossed the center line and killed my daughter.

ANGER

Annoyance, irritation, fury, rage, antagonism, resentment.

Opposite: calm

EXAMPLE: I had worked on that sales account and I needed it to hit my quota. He came in, smooth talked the client and walked away with my sale.

CONFUSION

Bewilderment, perplexity, puzzlement, mystification, uncertainty, misunderstanding, chaos, turmoil, muddle, mixed up,

Opposite: understanding

EXAMPLE: She said she loved me and then told me she wanted a divorce.

COMTEMPT

Disdain, dislike, disrespect, disapproval, scorn, hatred, derision, condescension,

Opposite: admiration

EXAMPLE: She will do anything, and I mean anything, for a buck.

SURPRISE

Shock, revelation, bolt from the blue, disclosure, bombshell, blow, shocker, astonish, amaze

EXAMPLE: I got 2 calls today. One from the IRS and the other from some attorney who said I had inherited an estate.

DETERMINED

Strong-minded, resolute, gritty, single-minded, unwavering, firm, dogged, indomitable

Opposite: irresolute

EXAMPLE: I was hungry but I had sworn to myself that I would not eat sweets anytime during the next 2 weeks.

SAD

Depressing, gloomy, miserable, cheerless, heartbreaking, distressing, heart-rending, poignant, moving

Opposite: cheerful

EXAMPLE: They posted the quiz results and my score was dismal. That means I failed for the year.

LYING

Deceitful, dishonest, two-faced, insincere, untruthful, mendacious, double-dealing, false, falseness

Opposite: truthful

EXAMPLE: I've never stolen anything in my life.

WORRIED

Concerned, anxious, apprehensive, nervous, bothered, troubled, vexed, upset

Opposite: unconcerned

EXAMPLE: The doctor said he would be right back after he looked at my test results. He's been in there a long time.

UPSET
Distress, disturb, sadden, trouble, offend, disappoint, disconcert, displease, grieve

Opposite: calm

EXAMPLE: They gave my promotion to Sally. My promotion!

HUMEROUS
Comedy, wit, funniness, the funny side, hilarity, absurdity, joking, jesting

Opposite: serious

EXAMPLE: My English teacher gave my report back and said I had missed a couple of periods. I told him no, we had always used protection.

DEFEATED
Beaten, overcome, overpowered, overwhelmed, conquered, crushed, routed, whitewashed, trounced, vanquished, subjugated,

Opposite: victorious

EXAMPLE: I don't mind losing a game or two but they said I couldn't play for my entire time I'm in school.

WINNING
Come first, succeed, be successful, prevail, triumph

Opposite: defeat

EXAMPLE: I had a hunch and it worked out perfectly.

SEARCHING YOUR MEMORIES

The most basic and simple tools any person can use to improve his or her craft and scene skills are LOVE and HATE. Happily, these two emotions are found in and can be used with almost any script.

Human reactions to these two emotions are more or less universal. Therefore, using one or both of these in a performance can be an excellent choice.

These two sharpened and finely tuned tools should be the first you put into your 'Plug-n-Play' art set.

Again, get into a darkened quiet place where you can let yourself float back to past memories from your life. Get comfortable. Close your eyes and breathe deeply. If you took notes during the previous exercise, refresh your memory of who, what, when, where and why and this time be more specific.

Who was involved?

What was going on?

When did this take place?

Where was it at?

How did it start?

STEP ONE

SEARCH <u>YOUR</u> memory for events or occasions where you felt LOVE. The stronger the memory, the better. You should identify a real emotion.

Be sure to picture the other person or object in your mind. If you have real pictures or a video of the person or object, use those.

Don't be afraid to use thoughts and ideas from your own life. The more important, vivid and deep the emotion, thought or idea of your love from your real life (past and present), the better and easier it will be to insert silently and seamlessly beneath an author's script.

I call this 'Lying (words of the script) with the full weight of the truth (Your emotions).'

If after several attempts you can't bring to your consciousness an event that expresses love, then skip it and go to HATE.

You can always come back to LOVE later when your mind has had time to silently search your memories. Given time, your subconscious mind will 'float' what you seek to the surface, usually when you least expect it. If it does float to the surface, quickly make a written note. Subconscious memories, like most dreams, are slippery fish and quickly return to the mental deep.

Most of us avoid pain (mental and physical). If a memory is a painful one for you, let yourself slowly go there in your mind and realize that it is exactly that pain that you seek to express in your performance.

Once you've learned how to let yourself go into a particular state of mind, you can just as easily learn how to get yourself out of it (or any other mindset) by deciding and choosing a different feeling.

STEP TWO

Once you've identified your memory of love, hate or each of the above emotions, and you are relaxed and in an unhurried atmosphere, let yourself relive each emotion to the fullest.

Who was involved?

Where were you, what were you and others wearing, how were you feeling, breathing, moving?

What were you and others saying?

What were you thinking?

In your mind bring the memory to life again.

STEP THREE

Privately write down an actual scenario from love, hate and each of the above listed emotions. I say 'privately' because again, these memories and thoughts can be painful, illegal, or embarrassing. Be brutally honest with yourself and how you felt.

These feelings should be deep within your consciousness so when they are inserted beneath the words of a script they will allow you to give a performance with a life of its own. Your performance will not be just some actor portraying some character. Your performance will be an actor becoming that character.

Take your time and give each item on the list truthful and serious consideration.

Later after the feeling of each of the items on the list has been committed to memory and internalized you will be able to destroy the paper trail.

Like 'weight training' start slow and proceed daily at regular and frequent intervals. You are not trying to win a race, you are building a 'Plug-n-Play' art set which you can use for the rest of your life.

STEP FOUR

Break down each memory into one or two words. These will be your **KEYWORD(S)** for each emotion or feeling on the list above.

Use real words or made up words, it doesn't matter. Any word, group of words, sound, or image can be used as long as it can bring you immediately into that memorized state from Step Three. Word(s) are preferred over sounds or images because unlike sounds or images you will always have instant access to them.

That is not to say that music and sounds cannot be valuable to you. If you have a smart phone and can download different songs or sounds that bring up the memories and feelings you want to use then go for it.

However, to start, use any of the above stimuli to open and internalize the memory.

Later, after you've strengthened and internalized the memory, you can work on a keyword or keyword(s) stimulus.

STEP FIVE

Use your Keyword (or other stimuli) to bring you to each of the above emotions and memories while vividly thinking and being in that memory in your mind and body.

Insert your memories under someone else's words.

For Example:
Let's say my keyword for LOVE was
WOMAN.

While using either my **Keyword** or the images represented by those **memories and feelings** I would deliver the line below out loud.

> The ball rolled to
> the edge and fell to
> the floor.

The above sentence was intentionally kept flat. It's not the words that deliver the meaning. It is the thoughts, feelings and other skills that convey the meaning.

It is estimated that approximately ninety-three percent (93%) of all daily human communication is non-verbal. That means most of what you're saying ain't coming out of your mouth.

Now you try it.

Deliver the following line with the feelings of anger:

```
The ball rolled to
the edge and fell to
the floor.
```

When first doing these basic exercises, most of us, myself included, have a tendency to over act (over the top). For the purpose of these exercises, use only your eyes and voice. Put your hands in your pocket or by your side. Don't contort your face into a monster. Don't move your feet.

Do this exercise over and over again. Do it until you can see the memory in your mind while you say the words. Don't act the words, just say them while you vividly think of the feelings.

How'd you do?

Was it fun?

If the results are not what you want, do it over and over again. The more you do it the better you will be at this.

Learning a new language is not always easy, and this is a form of language, considered by many, as the highest form of language.

Try this REAL WORLD experiment.

Without saying a word aloud to anyone, let yourself feel the emotions of anger; nothing lethal or excessively strong, but definitely anger. Use your anger memory to put yourself into that feeling. Once you've let yourself feel anger, get your significant other or friend or associate to comment or ask what is bothering you or what is wrong, all without you saying a word to them.

EVERYONE CAN GET BETTER WITH PRACTICE!

LOVE

You've written down your memory for LOVE.

Yours is a burning love, a love for which you would 'walk to the ends of the earth'.

This can be a person, place, idea or thing. It doesn't have to be tangible but your emotion about it does. Choose the most powerful thing from your life, the stronger your feelings about it the better.

This is not an easy task for most, but it is vital to identify what it is that you are passionate about, what makes your heart throb and your palms sweaty. There are many emotions a professional communicator must identify with but love is the most universal and potent. That is why it is perfect for being the first tool in your art set.

Once you've found your "Love", relive it over and over letting the emotions wash over and through you like a surging ocean.

Who was it? How did it start? Where was it at? When was it? Were you sweating, did you find it hard to breath? Was your heart racing? Did the feelings possess you? Did you feel empowered, helpless? Were you turned on sexually, mentally? Did you want to sing? Cry?

Do this over and over, dozens, hundreds, thousands of times. Do it so often that you can instantly go there in your mind and body on a moment's notice, any time, any day.

Distill that scenario, emotion, memory, or thought to one or two words that, when brought to mind vividly, will immediately put you in the state you were in when the memory was originally made.

For some, music, sound, images, or video can be a productive stimulus. Use what works for you. Later you can convert everything to internal mental stimuli.

After you've done that, and it has become second nature, read the one sentence dialogue below out loud putting all those LOVE feelings into it.

> The first time I saw
> her the moon was
> barely visible and
> clouds scudded across
> the sky.

Have fun with this and don't let yourself get discouraged if it doesn't come easily. You can do this if you practice and you can do this well if you practice often and a lot.

Try your new skill system on the following practice sentences. Have fun!

PRACTICE SENTENCES FOR LOVE

I was crying when the puppy walked up and nuzzled my face with his nose.

If he comes back, I'm going to kill him.

He smiled and suddenly I was in love.

Why does she make me feel so miserable?

Tell me you don't care and I'll leave.

She will chew you up and spit you out.

My husband knows me.

36

She sat next to me and I felt very uncomfortable.

I'm here and I'm going to stay.

Make a simple list of your keywords. As you build your 'plug-n-play' art set, you can practice each and every day, all within 15 minutes or less.

Scientists tell us that our thought processes are tremendously faster than our speech or reading abilities.

NOTES ON LOVE:

_____

_____

_____

_____

_____

_____

_____

HATE

The second basic emotion to add to your art set is the opposite of love: HATE

As you did with love, find what it is that you hate; what you would destroy and kill with atrocious loathing, or something that makes the dark side of you rise up in your throat and the veins stick out in your neck.

If you have trouble identifying and finding a strong hate in your past or current memory, then imagine what situation or condition would bring out hate in whatever memory that you are using for love. In other words, what is it that would flip your love into hate?

HERE'S A HATE EXAMPLE:

What feelings would you have if you were forced to watch some deranged person attacking and brutally mutilating a small helpless child just for the fun of it?

You do not have to perpetrate or witness a crime to imagine what it would feel like to see it, helplessly watch it or commit it. With practice and time you will come to know what turns your stomach and what would make you into a killer.

Again, this is not an easy task at first but it will get easier with practice.

CAUTION: Sending your mind into the dark places of your being can be very depressing and difficult to shake off. If you find yourself getting too low and depressed, go back to your prepared memory of LOVE.

After you've done your work on HATE and it has become second nature, you've developed a KEYWORD for instantly installing HATE into your mind and body, read the same one sentence dialogue below putting all those HATE feelings into it.

For Example:
Let's say my keyword for HATE was (*)UNT.

The first time I saw her, the moon was barely visible and clouds scudded across the sky.

PRACTICE SENTENCES FOR HATE

I care about her but if she tells them the truth, I will kill her.

I am here and I'm going to stay.

He's a liar, a damn liar.

So you're the one who screwed me.

She stole everything from me.

I hope he burns in hell.

And the cement dried slowly.

Don't ever do that again.

My wife knows where I'm at.

_____

_____

_____

_____

Nothing in the world is static, and rarely do people use only one emotion in their communication with others. Once you've worked with these two emotions and gotten these down a bit, try combining the two emotions into the same sentence. There is no right or wrong way.

You may not always have someone to practice your 'plug-n-play' art set with. If you don't have someone to practice with, use a picture or piece of tape on the wall as the character you are delivering to. After all, the real person you're thinking about is in your mind.

Have fun as you practice. From the time we are small children, we are taught to 'stay in line', 'don't make trouble', 'behave', etc., etc.

What is so much fun about acting (communication) is that you can be someone else and not have to, within reason, behave yourself. Students in my classes are required to have fun with their monologues and scenes.

If it's not fun, it's not worth doing. And for all of you negative 'Crankovitches' out there, please notice that the word is FUN not EASY.

YOUR VOICE

Have you ever listened to a movie or TV with the sound off?

If you've ever done that you obviously noticed that the performance loses some of its depth and not just from the absence of dialogue.   Sounds, be they dialogue, background or music, add tremendous amounts of 'queues' to a story or play.

Even silent movies use music to add sound to the images on the screen. There too, many good movie scenes supplement blurry or unfocused images as a visual for a strictly audio oriented scene.

44

Your voice is a vital part of communicating your inner feelings, thoughts and ideas to self and others. If your speech is monotone, flat and always at the same speed, your audience will soon lose interest and you'll lose your audience.

FIVE FUNDEMENTALS OF YOUR VOICE

Emphasis/ De-emphasis

Speed: Fast/ Slow

Pitch up/ Pitch down

Tone up/ Tone down

Volume up/ Volume down

You should practice all of the sentences in this work-booklet aloud.

Yes, learning to use new tools can be stressful. Remember to work for short periods with breaks in between. You'll remember more that way. And secondly, yes, you said it, have fun.

EMPHASIS

Did you know you can often change the meaning of an entire sentence by emphasizing only one word?

Emphasize or 'hit' just one different word within the same sentence.

FOR EXAMPLE: *I didn't say he hit her.*

The word underlined and in bold below is the word you should emphasize.

__I__ didn't say he hit her.

It was someone else who said that.

*I **didn't** say he hit her.*

> I deny that I said it.

*I didn't **say** he hit her.*

> Did he write it out or maybe text it?

*I didn't say **he** hit her.*

> You got the wrong man officer.

*I didn't say he **hit** her.*

> Maybe he just yelled at her.

*I didn't say he hit **her**.*

> You've got the wrong woman officer.

Practice the sentences in the above exercise hitting the different words and listen carefully to how you've changed the meaning of the sentence. I've added what I thought the change made but that is only my opinion, and you may find something completely different.

Once you've done this practice with emphasis, enough that it has become almost second nature, work on each sentence in the Love and Hate exercises doing the same thing. Choose successive words in each sentence and listen for new meanings and sub-text (inflective meaning). Be sure to deliver each line with full emotion and feeling behind it, letting yourself see in your mind the person or thing that originally caused you to create the memory.

SPEED

Now go back to the Love/Hate practice sentences, keeping the emphasis on each successive word but vary the speed with which you recite the sentence. Try to keep the emotion in the sentence also.

Don't be afraid to be hyper-expressive ("over the top"). You are in training. Work the exercise diligently; add and subtract speed liberally.

Does that also change the meanings?

By changing the speed, does the sub-text (underlying meaning) of the sentence change?

Write out the new meaning. By doing this you will start to develop an 'ear' for sub-text.

Next, try the exercise by altering the speed before and after the hit word. If the hit word is sped-up, then make the rest of the sentence speed down.

After you've had fun with that, use the opposite protocol: hit word speed-down and the rest of the sentence speed-up.

Does any of that change the sentence meaning or sub-text?

Take a break, you deserve it. Come back to it later. Have fun.

PITCH

WARNING: If you have any medical condition that will stress the vocal cords you should consult your doctor before doing any of these exercises.

Even if you don't have a medical condition that stresses the voice, don't do the exercise below too quickly or too loudly. You wouldn't want to walk into a gym and, having never lifted anything heavier than a coffee cup and try to pick up six hundred pounds of weight. Start slow and pace yourself.

The vocal cords are connected to muscles which shorten or relax, causing the vocal cords to tighten or loosen. The tightening and loosening is how you make different pitches of sound. You want to work these vocal muscles slowly at first and get them ready for the workout.

Start this exercise slowly with a warm up exercise.

A good vocal warmup is a 'Slider.'

A slider is **softly** singing an E with the highest pitch you can **softly** sing comfortably. Then while continuing to **softly** sing the E, slide the pitch slowly down to as low as you can comfortably go. Notice that the E will usually change to an O sound.

Then reverse the process and go from the O to the E.

By doing this, you have slid up and down the pitch register of your voice.

If you've never done this, you may have 'cracks' in your pitch register where you have to momentarily adjust your throat muscles and the smooth pitch slide momentarily stops.

These cracks are usually indicative of certain vocal muscles being weak and unused. With practice, many of those 'cracks' in your register will disappear.

Remember: anyone can improve with practice.

Now that you've warmed up, go back to the emphasize exercise. Keep the emphasis on the hit word but when you recite the sentence change the pitch up and down.

Next, mix it up. If the word you hit is pitch up, than make the rest of the sentence pitch down and vice-versa.

After practicing this for a while, try out the Love and Hate practice sentences, adding all of the ingredients you can.

You guessed it again: have fun!

TONE

Simply put, tone is sound quality. Is it smooth, rough, raspy, smoky, or any other quality you can think of.

Changing sound quality can be difficult at first, but with practice you can improve your ability to change tone. One of the easiest ways I've found to change tone is to change the posture of my neck, head, and thorax.

Start slow and proceed with your practice. Use all of the previous sentences to mix it up, and then try the ones below.

VOLUME

Match the volume of your voice to the room. The volume of your voice when delivering a line when you're 'miked up' in a film will be quite different from when you are on stage in a 500 seat theater. Practice with your voice at different volumes and in different rooms.

Be aware of how volume can change the meaning behind the words.

Speak the Voice Practice sentences below out loud. Use emphasis, pitch, speed, tone and volume on all of them. Mix and match all of the variables, and listen to your results.

VOICE PRACTICE SENTENCES

It doesn't matter.

I'm going to kill him.

I saw them with my own eyes.

I care about her.

She betrayed me and now I have no choice.

Do they really care?

They are already gone.

You said it was an emergency.

I am leaving.

Yes, I called him.

Everyone knows that but you.

He's a liar.

If they were there, they would have stopped him.

Who cares?

Now what?

I am not going.

Someone had to have tipped them off.

Both of them saw you with the gun.

My plan was perfect.

THE THUMB TOOL

If you've ever watched someone given a new script and asked them to read it without any prior rehearsal, it is likely that you will see the back side of the script more than their face or eyes. This is not good.

If there is more than one page to the sides, many, as they turn or flip to the second or third page will get hopelessly lost. This will require a few seconds or more to find their place. This causes a big break in continuity as they scramble to find their next line.

That break in continuity also destroys any emotional communication between characters doing the reading and between characters and the audience.

The method described below is designed to eliminate or reduce the time necessary for an actor to find his place in a script which he may have never seen.

When given a new scene to cold read:

1. Ask the person giving it to you if you can mark on it. Usually this will be okay.

Once you've got permission to mark your sides:

2. Take out your trusty marker or pen which you <u>always</u> bring to auditions, determine which lines are your character's lines, and quickly draw an outline of a thumb or a big easily seen mark of some kind in the left margin next to each.

3. Draw a thumb or mark **ONLY** next to **your** lines.

4. Memorize your first and last lines.

5. If you <u>start first</u>, put your left thumb beside your second line, look up at your reading partner and deliver your line.

If you <u>start second</u>, put your left thumb beside your second line, look up at your reading partner and listen to them deliver their line.

The physicality of moving your left thumb to the next mark, reading your line, looking up at your reading partner, delivering your line and listening to your partner's line between the first and second reader are opposite of each other.

6. It is important that you listen to what your reading partner is saying.

7. When your reading partner has finished his/her line, look down at your next line which is to the right directly across from your left thumb.

8. Quickly read it and move your left thumb to beside your next line which should have a thumb or mark next to it.

9. Look up at your reading partner.

10. Deliver your line.

11. Go to step 7 and continue between #7 & #11 until the scene ends.

At first, learning to walk or drive a car with a standard transmission is not an easy process. However, with practice (and more practice) you'll be surprised how much you can improve.

The golden key is Practice.

Before you start reading and listening, quickly read the sides making a decision of what this character wants and needs in this scene. What is this scene all about?

Wants and needs are your mechanical investigation of a scene. In the next chapter you'll get an easy method to remember these.

Chose one of your 'plug-n-play' tools. Feel the feeling that you've practiced with that memory. See the original 'person or thing' replaced in your mind with the other actor you will be reading with.

.

It cannot be understated how important it is for an actor to **Listen** and watch your scene partner while they deliver their line(s). Are you thinking of what your wants and needs are with the other character? Are you thinking of what the other character's wants and needs are? What conflicts are developing between your character and the other?

In an audition situation, where the person reading with you will probably not 'give' you very much (emotion) it is vital that you listen to their words.

62

You should always strive to keep the paper script low so that it does not block your face or eyes.

Also, at auditions you should always at least hold the script in your hand even if you have memorized your lines. This is an indication to the casting person(s) that this is an audition and not a final scene performance: unless of course the casting person(s) asks that you not hold it.

Try reading the following short script with someone to read with you. After you feel comfortable with your first reading, switch roles and try that.

Have fun.

Who knows? After practicing this and getting proficient at it, you might be able to walk and chew bubble gum at the same time.

START

JACK

What time do you want me to pick you up?

JILL

I'm working late tonight so... how about eight-thirty?

JACK

You're always working late. You do realize that today is Friday don't you?

JILL

What is that supposed to mean?

JACK

Just that you're always working late? What about us?

JILL

Us? There is no us.

JACK

Fine! Suit yourself. I just got my car
out of the shop.

JILL

Your car is a piece of crap!

END

TOP SECRET

The very first thing to a successful read, cold or otherwise, is when given a script, determine five things:

1. Who is your character?

2. What is your relationship to the other character?

3. What does your character want?

4. Why can't your character have what they want?

5. How important is this to your character?

Who is your character?

Your understanding and description of your character should be deeper and more than just 'a man named Bob'.

What kind of a person is he or she?

Is he or she straight, gay, quiet, angry, and boisterous?

Is he or she outgoing, withdrawn, intelligent, dumb, greedy, venal?

Think of all the nuances that go into making up a living breathing person. This character does not have to resemble your real life personality. The character characteristics can be quite different from yours. The choices of who this character is are yours.

What is your relationship to the other character?

Again, this should be more than 'my wife'.

If in the example of a married couple, where are they at in their marriage?

Newlyweds, sedate, comfortable, tired, bored, cheating, etc., etc.? Again the choices you make are yours.

What does your character want?

We all want something. Money, power, sex, acceptance, etc. All human communication is about WANTS and NEEDS.

You only communicate with someone else (talk, look, cry, plead, write, text, radio, phone, non-verbal, etc., etc.) when you want or need something. They only communicate with you when they want or need something from you (physical, psychological, emotional, and/or social, etc.).

What are your character wants and needs in this scene?

What are the other actor's character's wants and needs in this scene?

Why can't your character have what they want?

There is always something standing in the way of each character getting what they want and need. This creates a CONFLICT between your character and what they want and need.

Conflict is good.

Conflict attracts attention.

What stands in your character's way of getting what you need and want?

What stands in the other character's way of getting what they need and want?

Fight for what your character wants and needs. If everyone instantly got what they wanted or needed then the story would be flat and uninteresting. As an actor, don't shy away from wants and needs. Make strong choices of what you want and need. By doing this, you give your character a challenge and that will draw the attention of your audience.

How important is this to your character?

If I put a plastic bag over your head, would you find breathing pretty important?

Importance is again, your choice. The stronger the better.

NOTE:

The greater the CONFLICTS, the greater the IMPORTANCE, and the more juice or interest from the audience in the scene.

Don't be afraid on a cold read or audition to fight the biggest conflict, the most important conflict you can think of. As an actor you WANT to bring that fire out onto the ice!

70

In an effort to simplify the above five points to memory, I've associated them with the five fingers of my hand. Most of us will bring at least one hand to an audition, so in a pinch you'll have a quick easy reference to breaking down a cold read.

A Five Finger Actor's Checklist follows.

FIVE FINGER ACTOR'S CHECKLIST

1. Who is your character? (THUMB)

2. What is your relationship to the other character? (INDEX)

3. What does your character want? (MIDDLE)

4. Why can't your character have what they want? (RING)

5. How important is this to your character? (PINKY)

If the character wants and needs are not obvious or apparent in the written words of the script, it is your imagination's job to build and choose the most powerful wants, needs, and conflicts into the words as written. Since this is a cold read, delivering the proper words is nowhere as important as delivering a powerful communication meanings (wants, needs, conflicts and importance).

WHAT IF?

An excellent way to make strong choices is to do what I call 'What if?"

Below are the voice practice sentences again. After each one I've added 'What if?" statements.

Answer these 'What if?" as a back-story when you practice these sentences.

The given 'what if's are my 'what if's.' Use your imagination to come up with your own then repeat the sentence with your choice. Do the meanings of the sentences change?

Try to answer the five script questions about each sentence using my 'what if' back-story first. Then try it with one of your own.

WHAT IF?

It doesn't matter.

EXAMPLE

What if your sister is bleeding profusely from an auto accident and she wants you to let go of your direct wound pressure and get her phone out of the wrecked car? She'll bleed to death if you do.

THUMB: Who is my character?

I'm her older brother who just got out of prison.

INDEX: What is my relationship with my sister?

We've always been at odds with each other. She's prim and proper. I've always been in deep shit.

MIDDLE: What do I want from her?

I wish she'd just die.

RING: Why can't my character have what I want?

I don't like her but she's still the only family I've got. I don't want to be responsible for killing her.

PINKY: How important is she to me?

I'm flat broke and going to move in with her. If she's dead I'm out on the streets again and it's just a matter of time till I land back in the slammer.

I'm going to kill him.

EXAMPLE

What if 'him' is your father and he is the only person who can donate a kidney to you?

1. THUMB: Who is my character?

I'm the son he forgot. After he divorced my mom he married someone else and had a new son and family.

INDEX: What is my relationship with my father?

I think he's a prick. He doesn't come around, doesn't show up, not even a birthday card or 'how you doing?' I don't think he even knew I was alive until the doctors contacted him about my kidney transplant.

MIDDLE: What do I want from him?

I'd like to tell him to get lost again.

RING: Why can't I do that?

Because I need that kidney and I'll die without it.

PINKY: How important is he to me?

If he refuses to donate that kidney, I'll be dead in a month.

I saw them with my own eyes.

EXAMPLE

What if 'them' are your fiancé and your worst enemy and you saw them kissing passionately?

1. THUMB: Who is my character?

I'm the guy who always treated her like a princess. I put her on a pedestal. I got a job, a back breaking job, so I could get enough money to marry her, buy a house and a new car.

2. INDEX: What is my relationship to the other character?

Before seeing what I saw I thought she was better than sliced bread. Now I think she's a whore.

3. MIDDLE: What does my character want?

I want validation for everything I've done for her.

4. RING: Why can't my character have what they want?

If she is in love with this other guy then everything I've done, all the work and sweat, is lost.

5. PINKY: How important is this to my character?

She has been my entire life for the past three years. Without her, I won't have anything.

I care about her.

EXAMPLE

What if your mother wants to put a restraining order on you so that you will never be allowed to see her or any other members of your family again?

1. THUMB: Who is my character?

I'm the son who got mixed up with drugs. I'm the son who got potted out of his mind and pulled a gun on my brother in law.

2. INDEX: What is my relationship to the other character?

I always felt I was Mom's favorite. She always let me back in after I screwed up. Not this time. She can't even look me in the eye.

3. MIDDLE: What does my character want?

I want my family back. I'm lost without them. I'm living in my car and lonely.

4. RING: Why can't my character have what they want?

A leopard can't change its spots. They don't trust me and I doubt that they have any love or respect for me. They're serious.

5. PINKY: How important is this to my character?

I didn't know how important Mom and the family were to me until I lost them. Without them I just might as well go OD.

She betrayed me and now I have no choice.

EXAMPLE

What if your ex posted on Facebook explicit pornographic pictures of you masturbating alongside two other people of the same sex?

1. THUMB: Who is my character?

I'm a straight gal who drinks too much. When I'm drunk I lose control of my actions.

2. INDEX: What is my relationship to the other character?

I thought we were going to be married. We had a somewhat active sex life. He said I was a sex maniac. I called him 'queer' because he only wanted sex every other week. I told him to get lost.

3. MIDDLE: What does my character want?

Revenge! My 5000 Facebook friends saw that picture of me and my two sorority sisters. If I could catch him alone I'd like to wring his neck and break every bone in his hands.

4. RING: Why can't my character have what they want?

They'd lock me away in some cell probably with some dyke who'd want to redo the picture. I don't want him to know how much he's hurt me. I may be a slut but I'm too proud to let him know the pain I feel.

5. PINKY: How important is this to my character?

I find it hard to breath from the humiliation. My mother won't talk to me and the sorority has kicked me and my two friends out. If I had the money I'd put a hit out on him.

<u>Do they really care?</u>

<u>EXAMPLE</u>

What if your parents called the police about you and your suspected use of marijuana?

1. THUMB: Who is my character?

I like to get high. I don't hurt anyone. I want to do what I want to when I want to do it. I'm brilliant and smart. Who needs a high school diploma anyway?

2. INDEX: What is my relationship to the other character?

They're old and stuck in their ways. They've been on my back since I was twelve years old and they caught me smoking a cigarette. They just don't understand.

3. MIDDLE: What does my character want?

I want them to mind their own damn business. I wish they could just love me for who I am. I want them to love me.

4. RING: Why can't my character have what they want?

I hate them for calling the cops. Calling the cops on me sure ain't gonna make me feel warm and fuzzy about them. I hate them too much to tell them how much they've always hurt me.

5. PINKY: How important is this to my character?

I love Dad and Mom. Funny thing is I hate them too.

They are already gone.

EXAMPLE

What if you were promised a thousand dollars cash if you could find a certain package and bring it to the train station by 10 o'clock?

1. THUMB: Who is my character?

I started my own courier service. Things have been really slow getting started. I got bills to pay and I'm afraid my credit card company is going to send out a hit man for me.

2. INDEX: What is my relationship to the other character?

This guy came into my office and wanted me to pick up a package and deliver it to another guy at the train station by 10 o'clock. I missed the train. I screwed up. I don't like the way the guy looks. He looks as though he wants to break my legs.

3. MIDDLE: What does my character want?

I want him to understand that I got caught in traffic and missed the train. I want to be powerful enough to survive. I want him to leave my shop and not stuff me in a garbage bag.

4. RING: Why can't my character have what he wants?

This guy is angry because I missed the train. I didn't open the package but I've got a strong suspicion that whatever is in it is illegal.

5. PINKY: How important is this to my character?

I don't want my legs broken and I surely don't want to sleep with the fish either. I really hate pain.

<u>You said it was an emergency.</u>

<u>EXAMPLE</u>

What if you rushed over to your brother's in such a hurry that you are only partially dressed and your brother and friends are sitting around discussing football and drinking beer?

1. THUMB: Who is my character?

I'm the dutiful conservative twin sister of this bozo.

2. INDEX: What is my relationship to the other character?

Even though we are twins we couldn't be more different. My brother is completely wild and crazy while I like things quiet and simple. I'm always picking up after him and cleaning up his messes. I have been for all of my life.

3. MIDDLE: What does my character want?

I want my brother to understand that I have a life too. I don't want to spend the rest of my life picking and cleaning his shit. I want validation as a person.

4. RING: Why can't my character have what they want?

We're twins. We grew up together. I love him in a funny way. He will never change. He doesn't give a damn if I live or die.

5. PINKY: How important is this to my character?

I'm fed up with his antics. I'm going to tell him that I don't want him to call or see me anymore. I'm disowning him as my brother. Tomorrow.

Your turn.

Imagination is important. Don't be frightened to let your mind take you to exotic, weird, elusive, dangerous, magical places. That being said, use your imagination and fill in the wants and needs for the following statements and questions.

I am leaving.

EXAMPLE

What if you really want to stay and you want them to make you stay?

1. THUMB: Who is my character?

2. INDEX: What is my relationship to the other character?

3. MIDDLE: What does my character want?

4. RING: Why can't my character have what they want?

5. PINKY: How important is this to my character?

Yes, I called him.

EXAMPLE

What if the person you called is the one person in the world you hate the most?

1. THUMB: Who is my character?

2. INDEX: What is my relationship to the other character?

3. MIDDLE: What does my character want?

4. RING: Why can't my character have what they want?

5. PINKY: How important is this to my character?

<u>Everyone knows that but you.</u>

EXAMPLE

What if what everyone knows is that their spouse is cheating on them? With you. With one of their parents.

1. THUMB: Who is my character?

2. INDEX: What is my relationship to the other character?

3. MIDDLE: What does my character want?

4. RING: Why can't my character have what they want?

5. PINKY: How important is this to my character?

<u>He's a liar.</u>

EXAMPLE

What if the lies he tells are for their protection?

1. THUMB: Who is my character?

2. INDEX: What is my relationship to the other character?

3. MIDDLE: What does my character want?

4. RING: Why can't my character have what they want?

5. PINKY: How important is this to my character?

<u>If they were there, they would have stopped him.</u>

EXAMPLE

What if you know for certain that they were there?

1. THUMB: Who is my character?

2. INDEX: What is my relationship to the other character?

3. MIDDLE: What does my character want?

4. RING: Why can't my character have what they want?

5. PINKY: How important is this to my character?

<u>Who cares?</u>

EXAMPLE

What if you only have two months to live and no money for a life saving operation?

1. THUMB: Who is my character?

2. INDEX: What is my relationship to the other character?

3. MIDDLE: What does my character want?

4. RING: Why can't my character have what they want?

5. PINKY: How important is this to my character?

Now what?

EXAMPLE

What if you're being audited by the IRS, your significant other told you that you're too fat and wants to see someone else and your cat just had twelve kittens?

1. THUMB: Who is my character?

2. INDEX: What is my relationship to the other character?

3. MIDDLE: What does my character want?

4. RING: Why can't my character have what they want?

5. PINKY: How important is this to my character?

I am not going.

EXAMPLE

What if you've won a free trip to the orient and have waited all your life to go on a trip like this but your son has his first little league game while you'd be gone?

1. THUMB: Who is my character?

2. INDEX: What is my relationship to the other character?

3. MIDDLE: What does my character want?

4. RING: Why can't my character have what they want?

5. PINKY: How important is this to my character?

<u>Someone had to have tipped them off.</u>

EXAMPLE

What if the person who tipped them off is you and you're trying to point a finger elsewhere?

1. THUMB: Who is my character?

2. INDEX: What is my relationship to the other character?

3. MIDDLE: What does my character want?

4. RING: Why can't my character have what they want?

5. PINKY: How important is this to my character?

<u>Both of them saw you with the gun.</u>

EXAMPLE

What if the 'you with the gun' is the one person in the world that you love and would die for?

1. THUMB: Who is my character?

2. INDEX: What is my relationship to the other character?

3. MIDDLE: What does my character want?

4. RING: Why can't my character have what they want?

5. PINKY: How important is this to my character?

<u>My plan was perfect.</u>

EXAMPLE

What if the plan had a severe flaw which you did not anticipate and someone got killed over it?

1. THUMB: Who is my character?

2. INDEX: What is my relationship to the other character?

3. MIDDLE: What does my character want?

4. RING: Why can't my character have what they want?

5. PINKY: How important is this to my character?

USING MONOLOGUES TO BUILD YOUR ART SET

PRACTICE WITH TOOLS

1. Start slow

2. Build slow

3. Study friends, family, others. Study how they handle real life situations. Answer the five questions about the characters in each monologue.

4. Listen to family, friends, and others. Do their voices and posture betray their inner feelings? If the characters seem flat and uninteresting, imagine 'What ifs' for their background.

5. PRACTICE PRACTICE PRACTICE; Mix your emotional memories with what you are learning from watching and listening to others.

6. Search out monologues either in other books or movies and practice your craft with them.

MONOLOGUE ONE

I knew this can of paint was busted when I saw the puddle of green paint oozing out over the dining room table. My mother is going to kill me if she finds out about this. I just hope the paint isn't enamel and has to be removed using a solvent. The one thing my mom loves more than life itself is that damn dining room table.

Thumb:

Index:

Middle:

Ring:

Little:

MONOLOGUE TWO

By the time Ma Bell finishes with us, there'll be no place to come back to. We not the first of course, they've been doing it all up and down the west coast, all the way up to Canada and into Alaska. The bastards are gonna train 'em into some kind of half-ass sales force and use them to take over the whole damn communication system.

Thumb:

Index:

Middle:

Ring:

Little:

Think of it as if we're neighbors, and the only difference between you and me is there's usually a fence between us. That fence has all kinds of holes riddled in it. Some holes are bigger than others. I found one that was big enough for me to crawl through and there was some stuff I wanted to do, some creeps who needed to pay their bills... so... here I am.

Thumb:

Index:

Middle:

Ring:

Little:

As I was walking up the ramp I caught a glimpse of a shadow out of the corner of my eye and it sent shivers up the back of my neck. The complex had been full of workers most of the day but the last of them had left a long time ago leaving only me to pick up in the strange silence. It was chilly in there and I suddenly felt a powerful sense of foreboding within. But I wasn't alone. There was the shadow watching me from the corner of my eye.

Thumb:

Index:

Middle:

Ring:

Little:

It's hard to think of the gal as a murder suspect when she's a heart throb who could be on the cover of Vanity Fair, Cosmo or a dozen other magazines for those fortunate individuals with social graces and the luck of the world. However all of the victims were prominent men who were captains of industry and the type of men who used their money to go after women like her. Women who would never have to do laundry, or cook or mop floors. Check out her alibi for last Tuesday night and let me know where she was and who she was with. Ten bucks says the gal's is our shooter.

Thumb:

Index:

Middle:

Ring:

Little:

I'm the new attorney for Mister Wilson's estate. Mister Wilson's daughter did not feel that the previous lawyer, an weird little man named Emerson Sons, was knowledgeable enough to handle all of the complex transactions of Mister Wilson's numerous businesses. I know he was rather eccentric but there is also the question of questionable circumstances surrounding Mr. Wilson's unusual and untimely death.

Thumb:

Index:

Middle:

Ring:

Little:

Two families, both alike in social status, in beautiful Miami, where we start our scene, from a long forgotten grudge breaks a new war, where family blood makes family hands unclean. From the families of these two enemies, a pair of star crossed lovers commit suicide. The whole story is about mistake after mistake and how the kid's death eventually leads to the murder of both sets of parents.

Thumb:

Index:

Middle:

Ring:

Little:

PRACTICE SCRIPTS

SAMPLE SCRIPT ONE

START

ROSE

Such a pretty color. It'd be a shame
to waste it. What's it called?

MARIE

Verdant Green

ROSE

Do you have something we can store
it in?

MARIE

Use this empty salad dressing jar.

                    ROSE
        Have you got a funnel?

END

        Thumb:

        Index:

        Middle:

        Ring:

        Little:

            SAMPLE SCRIPT TWO

START

                    MARIE
        What are you doing?

                    BOB

What does it look like I'm doing? I couldn't sleep so I thought I'd get a little snack. I'm eating healthy- only salad.

MARIE
Turn off the lights when you go to bed.

BOB
I've got to tell you. This new salad dressing is really good.

MARIE
New salad dressing?

BOB
Yeah.

MARIE
What new salad dressing?

END

Thumb:

Index:

Middle:

Ring:

Little:

Thank you for working with me. I do appreciate the opportunity to work with talented people and I hope the stuff in this book will not only give you some tips to improve your acting (aka communication) but also inspire you to go for the brass ring and win the game. Best wishes for your journey.

REMEMBER:

PREPARATION

PRACTICE

And most of all:

HAVE FUN!

Printed in Great Britain
by Amazon